Union general, Ulysses S. Grant

Confederate general, Robert E. Lee

A paroled prisoner's pass approved by General Lee

Cornerstones of Freedom

The Story of

THE SURRENDER AT APPOMATTOX COURT HOUSE

By Zachary Kent

CHILDRENS PRESS ®

CHICAGO

General Lee and his officers overlook the battlefield.

Library of Congress Cataloging-in-Publication Data

Kent, Zachary.
    The story of the surrender at Appomattox / by Zachary Kent.
         p.   cm. — (Cornerstones of freedom)
    Summary: Describes the final skirmishes west of Richmond
which ended the Confederate Army's hopes of victory and depicts
the surrender at Appomattox and its aftermath.
    ISBN 0-516-04732-9
    1. Appomattox Campaign, 1865—Juvenile
literature. [1. Appomattox Campaign. 1865. 2. United
States—History—Civil War, 1861-1865—
Campaigns.] I. Title. II. Series.
E477.67.K46 1987   87-22468
973.7'38—dc19   CIP
                                                        AC

Childrens Press®, Chicago
Copyright © 1987 by Children's Press®,
a Division of Grolier Publishing Co., Inc.
All rights reserved.
Printed in the United States of America.

In ragged gray uniforms the weary Confederate soldiers tramped along the country road. Across the little valley at Sayler's Creek, Virginia, they marched in confused and hasty retreat on April 6, 1865. Suddenly, shrieking artillery shells tore through the air, and a rattling of riflefire broke from the trees around them. While Union cavalrymen galloped into their midst with slashing sabers, blue-clad infantrymen with fixed bayonets charged the startled gray column.

Some brave Confederates swung their muskets like clubs and struggled in hand-to-hand fighting. Most, however, panicked and tried to run away. Infantrymen threw their guns down and scattered into the woods. Frightened teamsters cut their horses loose, abandoning supply wagons. From a high ridge overlooking the battlefield, Confederate General Robert E. Lee watched the rout of his troops in disbelief.

"My God!" he quietly said. "Has the army been dissolved?"

Through the afternoon Lee and his officers pulled the remains of the Confederate army together. With

The Union army attacks the rear column of the retreating Confederate troops.

a last glimmer of hope the dignified, gray-haired general hurried his troops along the muddy roads leading westward. To one officer he admitted, though, "Half the army has been destroyed."

All day long the Union cavalry kept up the chase, never allowing the enemy to rest. At nightfall General Philip Sheridan triumphantly reported the success of his cavalry to Ulysses S. Grant, commander-in-chief of the Northern forces.

"Up to the present time we have captured ... several thousand prisoners, 14 pieces of artillery and a large number of wagons. If the thing is pressed," he excitedly insisted, "I think Lee will surrender."

Soon after, President Abraham Lincoln received a

copy of this hopeful message. Promptly he sent a note of his own to General Grant's Union headquarters. "Let the *thing* be pressed," Lincoln ordered.

No man in either the North or South wanted to end the fighting more than President Lincoln. Since 1861 the United States had been gripped in bloody civil war. A long raging argument over slavery had torn the country in two. In the North where factories thrived, thousands of European immigrants were willing to work for low wages. Most Northerners had no use for slavery and many considered it to be cruel and immoral. The South, however, depended upon slave labor for the success of its farming economy.

The 1860 election of Abraham Lincoln as sixteenth United States president brought the problem

General Grant received his commission as Lieutenant General of the U.S. Army from President Abraham Lincoln.

President Jefferson Davis and members of his cabinet

to its final crisis. Many angry Southerners feared that Lincoln, a Northerner from Illinois, planned to abolish slavery. Rather than submit, eleven Southern states quit the Union. Together they formed the Confederate States of America with Jefferson Davis as their president.

In April 1861 Confederate soldiers bombarded Fort Sumter in the harbor of Charleston, South Carolina, forcing the withdrawal of the Union garrison. The next day Lincoln called upon loyal troops to put down the rebellion. Soon the land shook with the crack of musketfire and the crash of thundering cannon. On a hundred battlefields with names like Bull Run, Shiloh, Antietam, Gettysburg, and Chickamauga, Union and Confederate soldiers fiercely clashed until more than six hundred thousand Americans lay buried in the ground. Although saddened by the bloodshed, Lincoln remained determined to hold the nation together.

At last after four long years, Lincoln found reason for hope. Union ships patrolled the waters of the Atlantic and the Gulf of Mexico, blocking Confederate trade routes. Union military victories on the Mississippi River and a thrust deep into Georgia divided the South into thirds. In several bloody Virginia battles during 1864, General Ulysses S. Grant's Army of the Potomac pounded its Southern enemy. Greatly weakened by these attacks, General Robert E. Lee ordered the Army of Northern Virginia to dig defensive trenches. A long network

Soldiers killed in the battle of Antietam Creek, September 1862

Union troops fire at Confederate soldiers who were ordered to hold their line from trenches.

of protective rifle pits and forts soon stretched from the Confederate capital of Richmond, Virginia, twenty miles south to the railroad center of Petersburg. During a ten-month seige the Union and Confederate armies fired at one another across fields of war-scarred no-man's-land.

While he waited for good weather, General Grant ordered his army of one hundred twenty-five thousand men supplied with fresh horses, equipment, and wagonloads of food. In the Confederate trenches sickness and desertion shrank Lee's ranks to less than fifty-seven thousand. Inspection tours along his lines reminded the general how sparse supplies were within his army.

"I've got no shoes, General," shouted a barefoot rebel soldier one day.

"I'm hungry, sir," another called. "We've got nothing to eat."

In spite of these hardships General Lee held his position until April 1, 1865. On that day Union cavalry captured the last rail line leading into Petersburg. Before the enemy could surround his position, General Lee ordered the trenches abandoned. On the night of April 2, Richmond citizens sadly watched the Confederates march away. Southern army surgeon James D. McCabe remembered, "At midnight the army commenced to withdraw from the trenches, and move rapidly . . . through the streets, towards the river." Rebel soldiers exploded arsenals

Captured Confederate fortifications at Petersburg, Virginia, 1864

A Matthew Brady photograph of Richmond after Union occupation

and torched warehouses until the flames blazed out of control.

By dawn the last of the Southern troops had fled westward across the James River. At the same time from the east Union soldiers invaded the burning capital. "Company after company, regiment after regiment," observed Richmond nurse Phoebe Yates Pember, "they poured into the doomed city, an endless stream." Squads of Northern troops doused the fires and patrolled the streets, bringing order to the ruined city. Most of the Yankees, however, chased the escaping Confederates.

On the roads winding forty miles to the west, broken rebel regiments retreated toward the town

12

of Amelia Courthouse. There General Lee expected to find waiting trainloads of food supplies. After feeding his men, the courageous Virginian hoped to march them south into North Carolina.

Exhausted and hungry, the Confederate troops swarmed across the countryside. South Carolina Lieutenant J. F. J. Caldwell understood the true condition of the Southern army. "The Confederacy was considered as 'gone up,' and every man felt it his duty . . . to save himself. . . . So we moved on in disorder, keeping no regular column, no regular pace. When a soldier became weary, he fell out, ate his scanty rations—if indeed, he had any—rested, rose and resumed the march."

The Confederate rear guard fought a running battle with the Yankee infantrymen behind them. To the south General Sheridan's hardy Union cavalrymen raced ahead, cutting off escape routes, capturing deserters and stragglers, and attacking rebel wagon trains.

When the Confederates arrived at Amelia Courthouse on April 4, they found boxes of artillery shells, harnesses, and other military supplies piled and waiting at the train station, but there was no food. Virginian John Esten Cooke observed, "No face wore a heavier shadow than that of General Lee. The failure of the supply of rations completely paralyzed him." In a drizzling rain the Confederate army pushed still farther to the west.

On the night of April 5, General Grant galloped to Jetersville to meet with General Sheridan. "Lee *is* in a bad fix," remarked Grant after examining maps with his cavalry chief. "It will be difficult for him to get away."

Excitedly General Sheridan swore, "He *can't* get away. We'll have his whole army."

On April 6 Northern troops attacked a large rebel column as it scrambled across Sayler's Creek. At one little bridge Confederate wagoneers whipped their horses as a hail of gunfire whizzed about their heads. Southern captain Fred Colston remembered, "One man next to me was struck, the bullet making a loud whack. We crowded on the bridge and . . . when I got across I looked back and saw the enemy setting fire to our wagons."

Stubbornly some Confederate troops stayed and fought to the death. Southern Major Robert Stiles witnessed "numbers of men kill each other with bayonets and the butts of muskets, and even bite each other . . . rolling on the ground like wild beasts." Bluecoat troops surrounded and captured as many as ten thousand stunned Confederates in the valley at Sayler's Creek. Taken as a prisoner, Southern General Richard Ewell sadly remarked,

General Sheridan moves his troops across Sayler's Creek.

"Our cause is gone. Lee should surrender now, before more lives are wasted."

Instead, the proud Confederate leader kept heading west with the remaining fragments of his once powerful army. Across the Appomattox River at High Bridge the rebel soldiers stumbled onward. At Farmville on April 7 the Confederates stiffly resisted a Yankee cavalry charge. General Grant commented, "The cavalry are doing very well. I'm hoping General Lee will continue to fight them. Every hour's delay lessens his chance of escape."

Grant entered the town on the heels of the retreating Southerners. He ordered General

Sensing victory is near, Union soldiers cheer General Grant.

Horatio Wright's troops to continue the chase through the night. Lieutenant Colonel Horace Porter of Grant's staff observed, "Notwithstanding the long march that day men sprang to their feet with a spirit that made everyone marvel at their pluck." When they noticed General Grant proudly watching them from a hotel porch, the men "seized straw and pine knots and improvised torches; cheers arose . . . with shouts of victory; bands played, banners waved, and muskets were swung in the air. . . . The night march had become a grand review, with Grant as the reviewing officer."

While these Yankee soldiers sensed complete success within their grasps, General Lee searched for a way to save his battered army. Through April 8 the jumbled Confederate regiments staggered westward another twenty-six miles to the little village of Appomattox Court House. Once again, however, General Lee discovered that food supplies had not reached the railroad station as ordered.

After a six-day march of ninety miles and constant skirmishing, Lee's troops now stood beside their bony horses or slumped upon the ground dazed and starving. Virginia colonel Magnus Thompson recalled, "The few men who still carried their muskets had hardly the appearance of soldiers—their clothes all tattered and covered with mud, their eyes sunken and lustreless..." From the east and north the gunfire of Union infantry crept closer by the hour. To the south, encircling Yankee cavalrymen filled the woods and roads, challenging all rebel attempts to escape. Under flags of truce General Grant sent several messages offering to accept the surrender of the Army of Northern Virginia.

By the morning of April 9, 1865, after a brief clash, Confederate General John B. Gordon, facing south with half of the army, instructed a messenger, "Tell General Lee I have fought my corps to a frazzle and I fear I can do nothing unless I am heavily supported..." Without enough men to fight a

Grant's official dispatch to the Secretary of War (left) tells of Lee's request for surrender (above). Surrounded by Union soldiers, the Confederate army (opposite page) waited as the terms of surrender are finalized.

winning battle, Robert E. Lee sadly concluded, "There is nothing left [for] me to do but to go and see General Grant, and I would rather die a thousand deaths." Responding to the Union commander's latest message Lee wrote, "I received your note this morning . . . with references to the surrender of this army. I now request an interview in accordance with . . . that purpose."

As soon as Grant received this letter he gladly ordered a cease fire along his battle lines and sent an aide, Lieutenant Colonel Orville Babcock, to arrange a meeting place. The popping of rifles quickly halted as white flags and murmured rumors of surrender flew along the opposing lines. In the Union camps roaring cheers and laughter filled the air. Confederate soldiers, however, learned of their defeat with the greatest sadness. North Carolina trooper Thomas Devereux noticed, "Some burst into tears, some threw down their guns . . . and I saw one man thrust his musket between a forked sapling, bend the barrel and say, 'No Yankee will ever shoot at us with you.'" News of the surrender stunned Louisiana artilleryman William Owen. "We had been thinking it might come to that, sooner or later; but when the shock came it was terrible. And was this to be the end of all our marching and fighting for the past four years? I could not keep back the tears that came to my eyes."

Early in the afternoon Colonel Babcock found General Lee resting beneath an apple tree in the Confederate camp. Slowly Lee rose and mounted his handsome gray horse, Traveller. Joined by staff officer Colonel Charles Marshall and an orderly, Sergeant G. W. Tucker, Lee rode with Babcock half a mile south to Appomattox Court House.

The sleepy little village contained the county court house, a tavern, several law offices, and a few stores. Colonel Marshall rode ahead of the others to find a suitable meeting place. On the street he met Wilmer McLean. Four years earlier McLean had owned a farm near Manassas, Virginia. During the war's first great battle at a creek called Bull Run, soldiers trampled his crops and cannonshells crashed

The McLean House at Appomattox Court House was the scene of Lee's surrender.

through his house. A year later, at the Second Battle of Bull Run, Northern and Southern armies destroyed his property again. In search of peace, McLean finally moved west to Appomattox Court House. Now, however, the war had found him once again.

McLean showed Colonel Marshall one nearby vacant house, but it contained no furniture. "Isn't there another place?" the colonel asked. Hesitantly McLean offered the use of his own two-story brick farmhouse. In a front parlor Lee, Marshall, and Babcock awaited General Grant's arrival, while Sergeant Tucker held the horses in the yard.

Past curious Union infantrymen General Grant and his staff arrived at Appomattox Court House. At the southern edge of the town they met General Sheridan and other gathered officers.

"Is Lee over there?" asked Grant quietly.

"Yes," answered Sheridan. "He's in that brick house."

"Well, then, we'll go over."

Grant rode his warhorse, Cincinnati, across the McLean yard, dismounted, and climbed the steps. Inside he greeted General Lee and soon sent word inviting his staff and other Union officers into the McLean parlor to watch the surrender. Colonel Porter recalled, "We entered and found General

Artist's version of the surrender at Appomattox

Grant seated in an old office arm-chair in the center of the room, and Lee sitting in a plain arm-chair . . . beside a square marble-topped table near the front window . . . facing General Grant." Colonel Marshall stood with an elbow resting on the fireplace mantel, as the federal officers quietly filled the room and stood along the walls.

Many observers noted how different the two generals looked. Reporter Sylvanus Cadwallader gazed at the gray hair and beard of fifty-seven-year-old Robert E. Lee. "Gen. Lee was older in appearance," he remembered, "but soldierly in every way. He was over six feet in height, rather heavily built in these later years of his life, neatly dressed in the full uniform of his rank, and wearing an elegant costly sword. . . . His manner and bearing were perfect, and stamped him a thoroughbred gentleman." Clearly General Lee represented the nobility of the Old South.

By contrast Ulysses S. Grant seemed to symbolize the simple people of the North. Colonel Porter recalled: "General Grant, then nearly forty-three years of age, was five feet eight inches in height, with shoulders slightly stooped. His hair and full beard were nut-brown, without a trace of gray in them. He had on his single-breasted blouse [coat] of dark-blue flannel . . . wore an ordinary pair of top-boots . . . and was without spurs. The boots and portions of his clothes were splattered with mud." Only lieutenant general's stars sewn on his shoulders revealed Grant was anything more than a common private.

Both officers had served in the U.S. Army during the Mexican War in 1847.

"I met you once before, General Lee," Grant now said, "while we were serving in Mexico. . . . I have always remembered your appearance, and I think I should have recognized you anywhere."

"Yes," replied General Lee, "I know I met

you . . . and I have often tried to recollect how you looked, but I have never been able to recall a single feature."

General Grant attempted other pleasant conversation, until General Lee gently reminded him of the purpose of their meeting. ". . . I asked to see you," he said, "to ascertain upon what terms you would receive the surrender of my army."

"The terms I propose," answered General Grant, "are those stated in my letter of yesterday — that is, the officers and men surrendered . . . and all arms, ammunition, and supplies to be delivered up as captured property."

"Those are about the conditions I expected," softly stated General Lee.

General Grant began writing out the surrender terms on paper. After gazing at General Lee's shining dress sword, he jotted the additional words: "This will not embrace the side arms of the officers, nor their private horses or baggage."

The written terms were passed to General Lee. Putting on his reading glasses he carefully examined them. Touched by Grant's generosity toward his officers Lee remarked, "This will have a very happy effect upon my army." After a hesitant pause he asked, "The cavalrymen and artillerists own their own horses in our army. . . . I should like to under-

Soldiers pose in front of the McLean House.

stand whether these men will be permitted to retain their horses?"

Grant told him that according to the written terms they would not, until he saw Lee's saddened face.

"Well, the subject is quite new to me," the Union general quickly added. "Of course I did not know that any private soldier owned their animals, but I think this will be the last battle of the war . . . and I take it that most of the men in the ranks are small farmers, and . . . it is doubtful whether they will be able to put in a crop . . . without the aid of their horses.

"I will arrange it in this way: I will not change the

On the day of the surrender, an artist drew this sketch of
Union soldiers sharing their rations with Confederate soldiers.

terms as they are written, but I will instruct the
officers . . . to let all the men who claim to own a
horse or mule take the animals home with them to
work their little farms."

"This will have the best possible effect upon my
men," gratefully responded General Lee.

While General Grant's secretary, Lieutenant Colonel Ely S. Parker (a full-blooded Seneca Indian),
wrote formal copies of the surrender terms, General
Lee remarked, "I have a thousand or more of your
men as prisoners, General Grant . . . whom we have
required to march along with us. . . . I shall be glad
to send them into your lines . . . for I have no provi-
sions for them. I have, indeed, nothing for my own
men. They have been living for the last few days . . .
upon parched corn."

Promptly Grant ordered beef, bread, coffee, and sugar sent into the Confederate camp to feed the conquered enemy.

Just before four o'clock General Grant signed the surrender terms and General Lee presented his letter of acceptance. Lee shook hands with Grant, bowed to the other officers and left the room. From the McLean yard Confederate colonel Armistead Long watched General Lee leave the house and cross the porch. Lee, he thought, seemed suddenly "older, grayer, more quiet and reserved . . . very tired." The Confederate general waited, lost in gloomy thought, until Sergeant Tucker led forward his

Following the Civil War, Lee was indicted for treason but was never brought to trial. Later he applied for a federal pardon but it was never granted. He died in 1870, not long after Ulysses Grant was elected president of the United States.

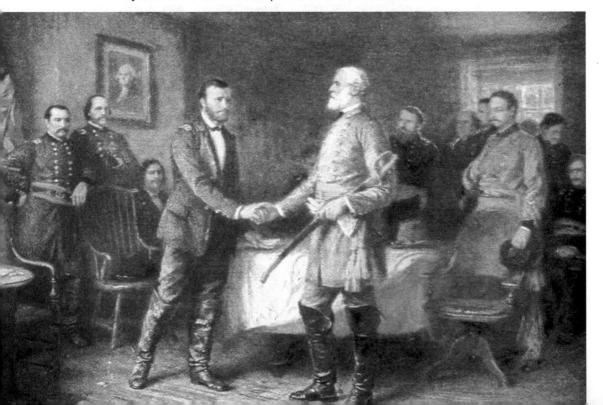

After the surrender, while newspapers (right) announced the terms of surrender, Lee rode back to his troops. As part of the surrender, Confederate soldiers turned in all firearms (except side arms) and ammunition. Rather than surrender their battle flags, however, many units burned or buried them.

horse. Mounting Traveller, Lee slowly rode off to the apple orchard where his army was encamped north of the town. Soon after, General Grant left for his own headquarters.

Inside the McLean parlor General Sheridan and other Union officers grabbed furniture and thrust money into Wilmer McLean's hands. Wishing to have mementos of the historic surrender, they rode off with tables, chairs, and candlesticks. While McLean protested the ruin of his house, other Yankees swarmed in and tore up upholstered sofas and broke up chairs, every man clutching for a little piece of history. Having witnessed the beginning of the war, McLean now unhappily witnessed its end as well.

Riding toward his lines General Grant heard Union cannon firing salutes at the glorious news of surrender. Immediately he ordered that this loud celebration be stopped. "The war is over," he kindly stated, "the rebels are our countrymen again." He saw no reason to shame the brave Southerners at the moment of their surrender.

Through the long afternoon General Lee wrote dispatches and oversaw the delivery of food to his hungry troops. At sunset, however, he began his last ride through his army's encampment to his head-quarters. As soon as the rebels saw their beloved general, they crowded the roadside to pay their final respects.

Trooper Devereux remembered, "As he approached we could see the reins hanging loose on his horse's neck and his head was sunk low on his breast. As the men began to cheer, he raised his head and hat in hand he passed by, his face flushed and his eyes ablaze."

Lieutenant Colonel W. W. Blackford noticed that tears trickled down Lee's cheeks and into his beard. "This exhibition of feeling on his part found quick response from the men, whose cheers changed to choking sobs."

"I love you just as well as ever, General Lee," loudly cried one grizzled soldier.

At his headquarters tent Lee briefly spoke. "Boys I have done the best I could for you. Go home now, and if you make as good citizens as you have soldiers, you will do well, and I shall always be proud of you."

On April 12, 1865, Lee's 28,231 remaining Confederates marched into Appomattox Court House between two long rows of Union troops. At "Surrender Triangle" where three roads crossed, these men piled their muskets and furled their battle flags in a formal surrender ceremony. Many soldiers wept as afterwards they started for their homes.

Only time could fully heal the war's bitterest wounds, but slavery was ended and the United States once more bound together. As rebels and Yankees trailed away from Appomattox Court House, Lieutenant Colonel Porter believed, "It was felt by all that peace had at last dawned upon the land. The charges were now withdrawn from the guns, the camp-fires were left to smolder in their ashes, the horses were detached from the cannon to be hitched to the plow, and the Army of the Union and the Army of Northern Virginia turned their backs upon each other for the first time in four long, bloody years."

PHOTO CREDITS

About the Author:

   Zachary Kent grew up in the town of Little Falls, New Jersey. He is a graduate of St. Lawrence University and holds a teaching certificate in English. Following college he was employed at a New York City literary agency for two years until he decided to launch a career as a writer. To support himself while writing, he has worked as a taxi driver, a shipping clerk, and a house painter.
   Mr. Kent has had a lifelong interest in American history. As a boy the study of the United States presidents was his special hobby. His collection of presidential items includes books, pictures, and games, as well as several autographed letters.